Dastak-Back To Back

Knock on your thoughts

AF518999

Aditya Kapoor

BookLeaf Publishing

India | USA | UK

Made with ❤ on the BookLeaf Publishing Platform
www.bookleafpub.in
www.bookleafpub.com

Dedication

I dedicate these poetries to all of those who have felt the love and care from someone, to those, who did not manage to express their emotions via their conversations or body language.

Keeping aside the gender based perspective and with a mix of Hindi and English poetry, I strongly believe that each and every word will touch your heart in some manner you must have had thought of at least once in your life.

After reading, I hope you get strength of understanding relations in a better way and will quote these meaningful lines to your loved ones.

Preface

As a free time hobby of randomly binding words together and creating a story within approximately 10-15 minutes of time, I do realize now, that it's not just a hobby to be named, rather its an artform of expressing your thoughts about life, love, care and feelings.

You would be able to relate to all of the lines written in context from an individual's point of view where I have tried my best to not only keep the momentum of rhyming words, rather I have made my best efforts to convey a story or a philosophy that should reach to masses bringing some positivity and provides you a different scope towards life through my words.

Acknowledgements

I would like to extend my appreciation to many people for being one of the reasons and part of process as they have been a true inspiration throughout.

No particular names to quote, though, once the book is out in their hands or via online platforms, people would know for whom these lines were written and even those by whose imaginary presence, it could have not been possible to fit in right words and sequential story telling with beautiful rhymes.

1. Daunting Dreams

You shine bright like a blossom flower,
Work hard to never fall
I know you have that firepower,
Your aura says it All

Every single time, when I feel Low,
I try to keep calm, and just watch you glow

Dream is to make you smile,
Make you mine, and achieve all goals with no whrine

All set to go as far you wish,
Hold my hand tight, and wait for a swish

My efforts are strong, but beliefs are stronger,
The day will come, proving that -
I belong to her
I belong to her

2. Be parwah

Kadr karte hain tumhari, mujhe sambhalna aasaan nahi
Galatiyan maaf kar dena, kya pata, maafi layak hain bhi ya nahi

Ruthe honge zarur , kabhi sahi to kabhi galat
Hasaane ke tareeke dhunde, gam dilaane ke nahi

Muskurahat tumhari kabhi khareed nahi paunga,
Itna ameer mujhe- bhagwan ne banaaya nahi

Duniya ke jese, ban to jaate beparwah,
Fir sun ne ko milta, jise chaha tha, ye vo to nahi

Esa kabi na ho, rone ki wajah ban jau,
Itni zurrat, mujh mein nahi

Parwah to bohot hai, mauka deke aazma lena
Lekin chook jate hain, kisi ne jataane ki kala, sikhaayi hi nahi

Aur jo jataa diya, uska kya mol aur kya faeda
Nibhaane ki taaqat
Har kisi mein nahi
Har kisi mein nahi

3. Memory Lane

Higher State of mind, of the nurtured kind
Makes me crazy, makes love blind

Watching you is the best time activity,
It isn't a choice really, it's the serendipity

The notebook of our lives, with limitless pages,
Turn by turn, page by page, shows emotions of ages

You the girl, sometimes sweet sometimes sour,
Still don't worry, I am on standby, waiting for my happy
Hour

Presence of yours been like photosynthesis,
Whether in happiness, or severe crisis

Your love strikes me with such intensity,
That I am left with only fidelity

We have made each other laugh so hard we have cried,

Surely we do feel each other's pain
When we are hurt deep inside.

4. Kuch Khaas Baat Hai

Maana
Maana insaan hu vesa, jiska kaam hi khushiyaan baantna hai,
Par meri khushi ka ho khayaal, isi ummeed mei mera jeena hai

Chah ke bhi na paas reh sake, usi cheez ka to rona hai,
Haqeeqat ko deke dhokha, kehna ke sang hona hai

Wahi sabh baatein hain zehen mein,
Jinhe soch ke dil bhar aata hai

Samajhna bhi zaruri nahi,
Waqt pyar mei, Yuheen badal jaata hai

Dekh ke bhi kia andekha,
vo rishte ki kuch baat hai

Jo na ho paaya bayaan honthon se,
Kaha ke vo jazbaat hai

Na jaane ab aur kitna, milega waqt humein saath hai
dilaasa dete hain hum aaj bhi,
Bas - ek raat ki hi to baat hai

5. Cup of Love

With your pretty little eyes, the magic you do,
Tell bundles of lies, I always get you

Like an eagle you flew, had your aim on sight,
Couldn't harm the one, he was brave inside

You tried so hard to keep yourself aside,
It surely didn't work out, was a bad choice

Like clouds you vanish in the middle of rain,
And chose the path with the hardest lane

It doesn't mean things won't get alright,
Have faith in me,

I'll always be standing by your side

I'll always be standing by your side

6. Kahani ka Zikr

Maang na paaya mai khuda se, Chaha tha maine saalon se kabhi
Aur mila vo aj jab dua ki rab se, Sirf ek vo dikhe, aur gaayab hon sabhi

Saathi ki na ummeed rakhi, Bas saath ki khwaish thi,
Taqdeer mein likha tha vo mile ese, Jese khuda ki numaish thi

Dheeme se, kaheen dur se, Duniya mein meri aana likha tha
Palat dia jeene ka saleeka, Jese do tarfah ek hi sikka tha

Kaagaz ke panno se, aage bohot dil jaa chuka,
Ye online rehna ab itna zaruri, Malum nahi waqt kahaan ruka

Thama vo jab, to saansein bhi ruki,
Ab na aur vishwaas kisi pyar par - Main bohot thak chuka

Dilaaya yakeen, aur fursat se samjhaaya,
Ye nahi gustaakhi dil ki, khubsurat aankhon ne rulaaya

Juta himmat , hua bharosa fir ek baar,
Kaha tha na jaana chor kar, Na bhar paunga mai vo daraar

Jab Bhi lage ke hoon akela, Yaadon mein tum kar lena mujhe yaad,
Paaoge mujhe tum saath sada, Aj nahi- to kuch din baad

Ginti Karna na kabhi, Waqt hua mulaakaat ko kitna,
Chah kar bhi na dur reh saku, pyar kiya tumko yun itna

Rakh paana zaara si himmat, vishwas vo jo bane misaal,
Parwah na kar tu duniya ki,
Rakhne ko main hun khayaal
Rakhne ko main hun khayaal

7. Connection

I will meet you next, and hug you tight
Kiss you my best and hold your hands till moon shines bright

We'll be smiling all the way, as we share our little stories,
We'll never fade away, as we're made up of those memories

Let's call it our heart's or mind's game,
No freaking idea- whom to blame

Kicking of anxiety, increasing of the proximity,
No fear of society, no wait of acceptability

I can see you happy and in Love, those are my strengths,
You bared with enough, no need to stretch it lengths

Set yourself - free for a while,
And see the magic mirror, when you'll smile

Think twice in your head, even if it seems a little cloudy,
Let those losers pay the bills, you walkout so much proudly

I wish I could say, come closer to me,
I would hold a rose bending on my knee

Waiting for the glory, of yours to shine,
And Say to everyone-
You are mine

8. Waqt ki Talaash

Ye jahaan ghoom liya samay bita liya, Kisi ache samay ki talaash mein,
Phir bhi vo sama na ban paaya, jiski humne kalpana ki thi, dekh ke aakash mein

Soch liya tha badal denge, kismat apni aaj se,
Ugta suraj kab dhal gaya, aur din beet gaya kaam kaaj se

Khangaalne lage hum sacchai, kismat ki lakeero mein,
Vo kismat hi to saath de gayi, hum gine gaye ameeron mein

Kuch log mile raaste mein, aur humne unka saath diya,
Par na jaane jab hum gire, koi na sahaara paas dikha

Ye rukha swabhaav dekh kar, man humaara udaas hua,
Beete hue un zakhmon par fir se thoda sa dard hua

Ab tak to hum jaan chuke hain, kesa ye samaaj hai,

Rakhna hoga khayaal khud ka, koi na rakhne wala laaj
hai

Ek pyar hi to hai Jisne, joda ye sansaar hai,
Varna, dekhane ko is sansaar mein, bacha nafrat ka
prachaar hai

Ek kiran ummeed ki jaagi, milkar tumko esa laga,
Maano saari sacchai jhuthi, aur ek tum mein vo pyar
dikha

Badal gayi vo soch puraani, Laga jese kuch khaas hua,
Tumse hi jaana kadr karna, ek zarurat ka ehsaas hua

Jis waqt ki talaash ka, besabri se kiya intezaar,
Vo waqt itna tezi se nikla, na hua humse vo izhaar

Chaha tha duniya mein mile, humko khushi sabse alag
si,
Tumse hi seekha asal mein, kese bane zindagi ajab si

Na jaane hum logon ko, kya hoga asar is baat ka,
Pyar se dar jab lage tumko, samajh lena, waqt hai
shuruwat ka

Sath dunga mai har pal, Jo himmat utni tumko dega,

Ke maangoge dua hamaari, aur vo jholi tumhaari bhar dega.

9. Appeal

Mighty Heart and mysterious eyes,
Would spend a minute, to get an incredible sight
Following the whispers, I get into my ears,
I love You!, Rolled down my tears

Pink nose and red cheeks, I could sense the shy in you,
Seems like a movie scene, a perfect day and sky being blue

Quivering lips of yours, may utter words of truth,
Bet, a few must have fallen for you, in their youth

Your hands so cold, holding warmth of mine,
Sets up the moment with some glasses of wine

I'll pull you through your waist, and wrap you around me,
Would feel like seconds, though, years spent so early

Little steps of your feet, taking a leap, into the deep sleep,
Wishing to wake up next to you, and YES, I'd feel I did a clean sweep.

Poking through your heart, hoping those feeling are getting on to you,
Cheers to this life and love we do,
This bond definitely makes a stronger ME and You.

10. Shayar-e-zubaani

Main keh to na saka, Kya hai is dil mein chupa
Kehna bohot kuch tha, magar kuch bhi na keh saka

Sambhal kar soch kar, gaur farmaaya to beshak,
kuch kehna to chaha, Magar bayaan na kar saka

Socho - Socho zara kya cheez ho tum, Tumhe iska ilm hi na tha,
Taareef karne chale the tumhaari, aur zubaan par ek lafz bhi na tha

Dekhte reh gaye vo aankhein tumhaari, aur zikr kuch to karna tha,

Josh to kaafi bhara tha dil mein, tamasha dikhana zaruri na tha,
Kya malum tha zariya badla sa aur zindagi mei kabhi - shayar ban jana hi likha tha

11. What you Are

You are my satisfaction, Something, I believe so strong,
Many a lies have come across, takes time to get along

Neither a dream, nor a reality,
Been a magical world, wished for our immortality

Still a dream to dream, seeing a joyful me with you,
We'll share our future, that's what I'd wish to hear from you

Could see the connection, you would not leave, I know,
Held my hand tight, promised to never let go

You've been the hiding place for a scared child, and,
The desire of hope, for the people to possess
Passed my tough times, with a demeanor of an Alpha,
Never felt it went all wrong, was supposed to care less

Being a pampered one, got lucky with the luck,

Who knew, what would I get, well deserved or really got
stuck

Stuck in your spirit, I was happy back then,
Don't worry, I won't step back, as,
I'm Your Man

12. Zaruri hai Kya

Rehene do zara kuch man mein,
Sabh kuch Keh jaana, Zaruri hai Kya

Rishto ko nazuk hi rehene do,
Sacchai ko jaanna, zaruri hai kya

Kuch hi to pal mil kar, jee bhar ke jee loge ,
Din bhar baatein karna, zaruri hai kya

Aur kitna zahir karoge khud ko,
Tere hi to hain, Duniya ko batana, Zaruri hai kya

Sab samajhte ho aankhon se, Jaan ho tum,
Bina kahe pyar kam ho jaega, Zaruri hai kya

Khud-b-khud, Sambhal jaenge sabh,
Ek ek ko alag se samjhana, Zaruri hai kya

13. A Child's Back-up

Finding the path, a child was born,
No sense of reality no sleeps until the dawn

Grown a bit, now he gets to see the world,
Hands still small, can't get to the things he'd wished he would hold

Being a child was enough to get attention,
Fulfilling all needs, surely was pampered-forgot to mention

Got scolding for deeds as main-course, some slaps on the side,
Rather preferred to keep quiet, else, took a situation slide

Soon realized he was still a child,
People around gave all of it, to keep it mild

Time came to be a man, leaving no mole,
Who would have thought, he carried an old soul

Closer to elders and wishful with kids around,
Mario was fun, always a winner with no rebounds

Got hit with adolescence, hit was hard to bare
Thought reciting loud and cycling were the reasons to scare

Voice was heavy, height was quiet cool,
Thought it would impress, kept flaunting like a fool

Now was the time again when reality kicked in,
Saw the world with my eyes first, strength came from within

Was always under father's umbrella holding my mother's hand
Never imagined, would have to face it and self understand

Carrying of the load on shoulders all of confidence stacked up,
Still a child resides inside, stating I've got my father as my back up

No matter how strong you become showcasing with your muscles curled,

Don't forget, who introduced you to this world.

14. Uljhan

Samjhaa naa Sako, esi uljhan naa bano,
Esa kon hi hai jo samajhaaye na samjhe

Uljhane itni bhi naa thi, naa thi samajh ,
Samajh-daaron ki kami nahi , vo khud-b-khud samjhe

Intezaar karoge? sabr rakh paoge?
Ye sawaal goonjata rahe kaano mein

Kalam zinda rakhna, agar alfaz hon khatm,
Na milna dukhi maikhaano mein.

Dua kabool ho na ho, dua karna na bhool jana,
Mushkilein hazaaro hi sahi, karm karna na bhool jana

Ye janam adhoora na rahe , Iska hisaab to rakh lena,
Rat gayi aur baat bhi,
Magar thoda sa dar upar wale ka bhi rakh lena

Suljha doge uljhe haalat kisi aur ke, to umar ghat nahi jaegi,
Zara sa aansu ponch ke to dekh,
Duniya teri sawar jaegi

15. As Strong as You can

You are the one you imagine into,
So you imagine what you think of yourself

You can conquer you knew,
Yes you heard it right-Don't act like deaf

Stop sulking anyway, you become the wall.
And let go off your weakness, you swear for it

World is full of obstacles, and same for all,
No need of any special harness for you to bare it

You'd ask for support, you have got it from me,
I can be the divine power, or whatever you want me to be

Have to have faith, that is all what's in need,
Can't really build a tree house, without growing that seed

Don't let it become a fireball,
Don't wait for it to burst on you,

Promise you'd make a mark in your mind after all,
You're never just one, will always have strength of two.

16. Kho Gaye Jazbaat

Chehere ki jagah ab 'Screen' kaafi hai,
Baaton ki jagah ab 'seen' hi baaki hai

Hansi ab 'emoji' mei dikha dete hain,
Aur aansu 'Wi-fi' mein beh jaate hain

Dil ki baat ko status update, aur aadmi ummeed mei jee raha hai,
Kisiko fark nahi jazbaat hain bhi ?- ya insaan andar se mara hai

Kese Ho? Theek bhi ho ya nahi ? ab type nahi karte,
Bas LIKES mein apnaapan khojte firte

Pehle to khat mein jazbaat ki izzat thi, aur aj bhi kimat hai,
Ab chat mei typing.., ka intezaar, yahi kismat hai

Rishte ab Online Reh jaate hain,
Aur Dil aksar offline reh jaate hain

Saath baith kar chai peena kahaan,
Ab video call mein sukoon sa dikhta hai wahaan

Dil ki dhadkane, vo aankhon ki baat,
Sabh kuch gum, sabh kuch ab bas yaad

Waqt shayad apno ke saath bita sakte the, ye hum sab jaante hain,
Magar vo to hum, jaane-anjaane mein 'Reels' aur 'Scroll' karne mein baha dete hain

Khud ki taareef, aur bhagwan se shikaayat karte hain tanhaai ki,
Gaur karoge to samjhoge, bina fal ke ped ko kosna to aasaan tha,
Magar hum jadon ko khud hi sukha dete hain

17. Fragrances of moments

In whispers of the past, I search for you,
A fleeting scent that dances anew.

Beete lamho ki mehek, a fragrance so true,
Lingers on my skin, a memory or two

Like autumn leaves, moments fall and fade,
Yet in their wake, a sweet aroma's made

The perfume of love, a whispered promise kept,
In every breath, my heart weeps and sorrows slept

In dreams, I see your smile so bright,
A flash of joy, a moment's light

Though time may steal our moments dear,
Their fragrance remains, always near

The scent of memories, a bittersweet refrain,
Echoes of love, a lingering pain

Yet in this fragrance, I'm lost again,
In beete lamho ki mehek, my heart's terrain

18. Ameeri

Asal mein ameer kaun hai ?

Kya ameer vo jise dhan bharaa ho, Ya Jiske paas mehel sunhera ho,
Ya vo jo har dil mein basta hai, Jo muskaano mein jiya karta hai

Kya ameeri hai shauhrat bhaari, Ya gaadiyon ki lambi kataari,
Ya fir vo jo waqt baanta hai, Aur har dukh mein saath chalta hai

Jiski baton mein mithaas hoti, Nazarein jhuki, par soch badi hoti,
Jo khud se pehle auron ki soche, Asali ameeri usmein hi to hoti

Jise naa ho abhaav ka dar, Na dil mein ho koi zeher,
Jiske paas santosh ka khazaana, vahi hai asali rayees-deewana

Na sona na chaandi, na hi taaj, Na naam na audha, na hi samaaj,
To mat dekho jeb ki geharaai, Dil ki daulat hai - sacchi kamaai

19. They Knew We'd Leave

They never asked for much from us,
No trophies, thanks, or grand applause.

Just showed up – calm, a guiding flame,
Who saw our spark before our name?

With patient eyes, they stood so near,
In moments loud, and those unclear.

They didn't lead with loud commands,
But with belief – and open hands.

They taught us more than lines and charts,
They stitched their truth into our hearts.

And when we fell, they never frowned,
Just waited while we found our ground.

We thought they'd always walk along,
That they'd be there our whole life long.

But mentors know — they never cling,
They give you roots, then give you wing.

One day we left, full-grown and bold,
Chasing dreams we longed to hold.

And they just smiled — not a goodbye,
But something softer in their eye.

Now years have passed, and here we stand,
With stories shaped by their own hand.

And in the quiet, late at night,
We hear their words still burning bright

20. Bhai Chaara

Pehli mulaakat mein the strangers jese kuch log,
Thodi hansi, thodi baatein, fir chal pada fun ka dose

Kabhi food ki debate, kabhi Chai breaks,
Hum sabko Samajh aa gaya, life is all about one take

Canteen ki bench pe chalti thi apni court,
Jaha judgement funny, aur laughter full on sport

Hansi ke case, and teasing ki sunwaai,
Aur saza- parantha tu khila, aaj teri baari aayi

Time nikla, aur bonding ho gayi strong,
Laatein khaai b'day pe, rona allowed ni, lekin bum bana dia kingkong

Koi gym to koi party, sabhke apke shauk khaas,
Warden se chupa bottle to le aaye, excitement mein sabh bhule glass

Hangover poora aur attendance kam,
Mazdoori lagti thi, vo classes lagaane ka gum

Ek ki awaz ke "Ghumne chalega bhai?"
Aur dusri aawaz "Bas shoes hi pehen raha hu bhai"

Mushkil se milte hai kuch pal sath bitaane ko yun hi,
Kuch phone mein busy, Kisi ko kaam ki majboori

Dosti bhul jana magar pyar na bhulna, varna teri kutaai hai
Dosti kab ki khatam, arre- tu to mera bhai hai

21. Talking to the Humans

I'm a doorway to the unknown, a path to secrets untold.
A mysterious person knocks on me, and I start to unfold.

My old framework shines with a soft light, like a warm and cozy beam.
The air around me hums with an otherworldly energy, like a gentle stream.

The person who knocked on me takes a step back, eyes wide with wonder.
They see a glimpse of what's beyond me, and their heart starts to thunder

.

I crack open, and a golden light pours out, like a sunrise in the morning.
It's an invitation to enter, to explore the mysteries that I'm storing

.

A whisper in the wind says, "Come and see, what's on the other side."
It's a call to the brave, to step into the unknown, and let their spirit glide.

I'm a threshold to a new world, where the ordinary and magical meet.
I'm a doorway to the infinite, where dreams and secrets are waiting to greet.

So, come and open me, and you shall see,
A world of wonder, where magic and mystery are set free
.

I'm The Mystical Door, and I'm here to show you the way,
To a place where anything is possible, and the impossible becomes the day.